DOUGLAS D

AUSTIN J. BROWN

First published 1993

ISBN 0 7110 2183 X

Published by Ian Allan Ltd, Shepperton, Surrey; and printed in Great Britain by Ian Allan Printing Ltd, Coombelands House, Addlestone, Surrey KT15 1HY

Previous page:
A splendid portrait of the Aces High Dakota G-DAKS taken in April 1983 whilst flying out of Duxford. Following its appearance in the film *Airline*, it was painted as KG374/YS-L to represent the No 271 Squadron aircraft flown by Flt Lt David Lord, DFC, who lost his life whilst flying a re-supply mission to Arnhem on 19 September 1944, and for which he was posthumously awarded the Victoria Cross. The aircraft now resides at North Weald disguised as TS423, and is still owned by Aces High. *Stephen Piercey (SP)*

Introduction

My first flight ever was on an Aer Lingus Viscount out of Manchester Airport in the summer of 1959, travelling on an exchange visit to Germany. A month later I came home to Newcastle, via Amsterdam, as an unaccompanied minor on a delayed night flight on board a Silver City DC-3. That sold flying to me at the age of 11, and I have had a particularly soft spot for the Dakota ever since. When Cambrian Airways sponsored me to become a pilot in 1966, mine was the first course to go directly on to the Viscount 701, missing the opportunity to fly their DC-3s by a hairsbreadth. So it was, when I left Cambrian/British Airways in 1977, that I went to Air BVI in the West Indies to fly the Dak at last, clocking up almost 1,000hr on it before coming home.

Did Donald Douglas realise what he was creating way back in 1935 when he built the DC-3, I asked myself as I flew VP-LVH down to Antigua from Tortola through its 65,000th hour one June day in 1979? That's about 8,500,000 operational miles! And it continued to fly for another 10 years. The aircraft with the highest time on it reputedly has flown over 90,000hr since it rolled off the production line on the 23 October,1937. What an achievement!

Left:
ZA947 climbs steeply away from the IAT meet at Fairford in Gloucestershire at the end of the show in July 1991, *en route* to its base at Farnborough. Operated by the Royal Aircraft Establishment, now known as the Defence Research Agency, it sports the highly visible 'raspberry ripple' colour scheme worn by all its aircraft. Built in 1943, it served with the Royal Canadian Air Force as '661', and became KG661 with the RAE at West Freugh. It was realised only in 1979 that the serial had been duplicated with another Dakota which had crashed on take-off at Crosby on Eden in 1944, so it became ZA947. Hence the modern serial. *AJB*

Front cover:
The Confederate Air Force's R4D-6S 'Ready 4 Duty' keeps close formation with us *en route* from Eindhoven to Amsterdam in July 1985, the DC3's 50th anniversary year. *Austin J. Brown (AJB)*

Back cover:
Seagreen Air Transport's C47B-DK sparkles in the Caribbean sunshine at V. C. Bird International Airport, Antigua, in March 1985. *AJB*

The DC-1 (Douglas Commercial One) was designed and built in response to a crying need for a safe, all-metal airliner, which would replace the weaker, wood and fabric types that the airlines were forced to operate at that time. Boeing was pressing ahead with the new Boeing 247 in concert with United Airlines, whilst TWA (then Transcontinental & Western Air), their main rival, was looking to Douglas to provide them with the answer to all their problems. The DC-2 was the designation of the refined, higher-powered production model which eventually went into service with TWA, followed by Pan American, Eastern and American. One hundred and ninety-three were built.

The DC-3 came about because of a requirement by American Airlines to replace its Curtiss Condors on their transcontinental routes. Passenger appeal was falling because the competition was now flying the faster DC-2, but the DC-2 could not accommodate their sleeper seats as its fuselage was too small. Between them, the Douglas Sleeper Transport (the DST) was evolved. This became the DC-3.

Some 600 DC-3s were built for the airlines, but the advent of World War 2 dictated that the type was impressed into military service, and 10,000 more were built specifically as C-47 Skytrains and C-53 Skytroopers. Later, they were also built under licence in Japan and the Soviet Union, where it became known as the Lisunov Li-2, powered by indigenous engines. The production lines ran in the States at Santa Monica, Long Beach and Oklahoma City between 1935 and 1946, but little is known about Japanese or Soviet production, other than that about 500 were built in Japan and about 2,000 in Russia. Many of the Soviet Li-2s found their way into China, where they flew for for CAAC, the nationalised airline.

To fly, the 'Old Lady' commands respect. You don't finish flying it until the chocks are under the wheels. Having been brought up on spamcans with nose-wheels, the DC-3 was my first taildragger. I had been trained to graduate to the Viscount from the start, an aircraft with very little ground clearance on the propeller tips, especially with the oleos fully compressed; 7in and 13in on the inboard and outboard props respectively to be exact! So, in the case of a crosswind landing, you could not afford to dip your upwind wing too much into the wind without the danger of clipping a prop and hearing expensive noises. I was, therefore, taught to crab in down finals, flare, wings still level, but with drift still on, and then kick it straight just before touching down, putting forward pressure on the elevator to gain positive nose-wheel adhesion and using nose-wheel steering and rudder to control the landing run and keep the aircraft straight. When I moved on to the BAe One-Eleven and adopted this method of landing, I found a tendency for the upwing wing to rise slightly, partly because of the swept wing, which is not to be recommended. 'Just like the Dak, old boy,' I was told, 'dip the wing into wind'. The trouble was, I'd never flown the Dak! Must do something about that one day, I thought. The C-47 has got such small ailerons that their effectiveness decreases greatly with loss of airspeed, so you can dip your wing into the crosswind with confidence.

In the early days, DC-3s were three-pointed on to the ground as the brakes were not as effective as they are today. The drag of the airframe was used to slow the aircraft down over the runway. Nowadays, with modern brakes, they are landed on the main wheels, braked, and the tail allowed to drop against forward pressure on the control column. Beef Island, in the Virgin Islands was an ideal training ground for landings, as it was possible to have winds from three different directions at various points on its short runway, with water at both ends to remind you that this wasn't a rehearsal.

You also needed some feeling in your feet, too, unlike so many modern tricycle gear types. To catch any possible swing on take-off, either wind or power induced, you had to 'walk' the rudders, as this way you can react to unexpected pressure and oppose it quicker than if your feet were at rest. Otherwise, it's like any other aircraft to fly. Terribly sedate, though, in the cruise, as it rides the currents of air; none of this cobblestone effect that wears out your back in a jet!

Forty-seven years since production ended, it is estimated that as many as 1,500 'Gooney Birds' are still flying or flyable throughout the world. I feel that the number has declined, though, at a greater rate during the last 10 years, partly because of the cost of Avgas over turbine fuel, and partly through spares, especially engine spares, becoming difficult to rely on. Turbine engines have now become so reliable that the certificating authorities are considering or even allowing single-engined IFR operations to take place, and the piston-engine's days are numbered in scheduled operation. However, not to be left out in the cold, and working on the principle that the only replacement for a DC-3 is another DC-3, some airframes have been re-engined with turbo-props. The basic airframe will take it as the frame is so strong. Warren Basler has gone farther than anyone to date with his Turbo-67, which is not just a modification but a complete rebuild of the airframe. His production line at Oshkosh, Wisconsin produces a fine aircraft, combining the qualities of the DC-3's inherent design with modern powerplants and instrumentation.

So, 1995 will be the 60th anniversary of that first flight of the prototype from Clover Field on the 17 December 1935. Plans are afoot not to let it go unnoticed. The Dutch Dakota Association aren't hedging their bets either; they're mothballing one to fly on its 100th birthday!

Austin J. Brown
Ealing
January 1993

ACKNOWLEDGEMENTS:

Thanks are due to the following friends: Steve Piercey, who infected me with Propliners, and his mother and father, Patsy and Ray, who passed over some of his collection to my Library, Arthur and Audrey Pearcy of Douglas DC-3 Survivors fame, John and Maureen Woods of the Friends of the DC-3, Mike Collett, James Foden, and all the guys at Air Atlantique, as well as Malcolm and Jean Stride, Rob Hewson and Eric Wagner for their moral support.

The photographs in this book have all been shot on Kodachrome 64 and Fujichrome Professional film using Nikon and Hasselblad equipment.

G-AOBN is a C-53D which flew with Air Anglia until the type was replaced within the company by the Fokker Friendship. It is seen here parked with the locks in, on the apron at Birmingham in May 1975. The aircraft was eventually sold to Ethiopian Airlines in July 1977 as ET-AGR. *SP*

Left:
G-AMPO has operated with no less than 16 companies in the UK since it left the RAF in 1952. Built at Oklahoma City, it joined the USAAF as a C-47B in 1945 and was transferred over to the Royal Air Force later that year, taking part in the Berlin Airlift with No 53 Squadron. I remember it with such famous companies as Starways, Eagle, British Westpoint, Intra and Eastern Airways, and even saw it operating on its one and only overseas lease to Polaris Air Transport as LN-RTO during 1965. Photographed here in the colours of Macedonian Aviation in 1974, it is now being rebuilt as a sprayer with Atlantic Air Transport at Coventry for the company's oil pollution contract with the Department of Transport.
SP

Below left:
Recently repainted in the company's new colours, Intra's C-47B taxies out to the holding point of Runway 27 at Jersey in August 1977. Intra operated six DC-3s at one point, later introducing the Viscount 700 to increase capacity. *SP*

Right:
Seen chasing across the Oxfordshire landscape from its base at Chalgrove, Steve Piercey photographed Martin Baker's Dakota G-APML just prior to its retirement in September 1981. It had been with them for 23 years, and was sold on to Air Atlantique, who used it for spares. *SP*

G-APML

Right:
Air Atlantique took over the pollution control contract from Harvest Air, and with it, the company's aircraft. Three of their DC-3s stand in the winter sunshine at Coventry during December 1992, ready for duty. In the background, parked on the cross-runway, is the Instone DC-6A G-APSA. More memories! *AJB*

Inset:
G-AMPZ wore this striking high visibility colour scheme when it worked for Harvest Air on the Ministry of Transport pollution control contract in the mid-1980s. Along with its stablemate G-AMYJ, it was fitted with spray bars for oil slick dispersion, and was on 24-hour standby to fly anywhere in the UK. It was photographed here at Exeter in November 1986. *AJB*

POLLUTION CONTROL
DEPT OF TRANSPORT
G-AMPZ

Left:
Even with 'Air Luton' titling showing through beneath the 'Top Flight' lettering, the multi-coloured wraparound bands give this Dakota away as being one of the Air Atlantique machines. G-ANAF was resting between career moves at Exeter in April 1986 whilst Top Flight's affairs were being sorted out, and now it's back in harness again with Air Atlantique. *AJB*

Right:
The 50th anniversary of Northwest Airlines in 1986 led to G-AMPY being painted up in Northwest's original colours for the air display season. Carrying the registration NW21711, it was caught here at the Northwest Anniversary Air Display at North Weald having a quiet word with one of its other surviving contemporaries, the Spitfire MK VIII MT719/YB-J.
AJB

YB • J
HWEST
NORTH

Air Atlantique
John Turnbull

Left:
'Charlie Alpha' gleams under the floodlights of Liverpool's apron on a night mail turnround in March 1987. *AJB*

Above right:
The Basler Turbo-67 conversion is not just the latest in a line of turboprop conversions, but a complete rebuild of the airframe during which the fuselage is lengthened by 1.02m forward of the wing centre section. N96BF is a regular globetrotter, photographed here on a demonstration flight with Air Atlantique at Coventry in March 1991. It was back at Farnborough for the show in September 1992. The DC-3's airframe is remarkably strong, and has been fitted with turboprops on many different occasions, the most notable being the BEA Dakotas fitted with Rolls-Royce Darts in the 1950s, when they operated high-speed freight services, and Jack Conroy's Tri-Turbo Three which operated until recently in the Arctic. *AJB*

Right:
Another Stephen Piercey shot of G-AMPO, here still in the basic colours of Eastern Airlines but wearing the titles of its new owner, Air Atlantique. Taken in the skies of mid-Wales in May 1982, it still operates for them 10 years later. *SP*

09-27

Left:
The Atlantique Dakota G-AMSV is marshalled into position on arrival at the International Air Tattoo at Fairford in July 1987, having given yet another group of enthusiasts the chance of flying in this 45-year old aircraft, which had accumulated some 35,000hr on the airframe when this picture was taken. *AJB*

Right:
Like a horse looking over a gate, the ex-Top Flight Dakota G-ANAF peers over the tail of G-AMHJ. They were parked at Exeter in November 1986 after Top Flight sank into receivership. Both are currently with Air Atlantique at Coventry.
AJB

40
T3-40
792
2
G-BFPW
744
51

Left:
A number of ex-Spanish Air Force C-47s arrived at Blackbushe in the summer of 1978, to be sold on soon afterwards. This one, temporarily registered G-BFPW, went on to the United States as N3753N, whilst most of its companions went to the Yemen. *AJB*

Right:
Clyden Airways, who were based in Dublin, took this Dakota into service in October 1978, and is seen here during engine runs at Exeter prior to delivery. It was restored to the British register as G-AKNB in January 1982. Well-known in the UK following its wartime career in the RAF, it flew many hours successively with BEA, Silver City, BUA and Intra, it continued with Harvest Air on its return from Ireland, but was damaged at Squire's Gate on 27 September 1982. Put on static display after that at Duxford as FD789, it was re-activated for the film *War and Remembrance* in December 1986, following which it was sold in the United States. *AJB*

NAPLES
BOSTON AIRLINE
N33PB

VIRGIN ISLANDS INTERNATIONAL AIRWAYS
N101RP

Left:
Photographed landing at Miami International during February 1978 on one of its frequent flights to and from Naples, Florida, this Douglas C-53 of Provincetown-Boston Airlines spent some of its life with Pan American after being de-mobbed by the USAAF in 1944. (AJB)

Below left:
One of the Virgin Islands International DC-3s lifts off the runway at St Thomas *en route* to San Juan, Puerto Rico, in March 1985. San Juan International is the gateway where the commuters meet the large carriers who cannot land at the smaller airports in the Caribbean chain. N101AP is one of a pair of aircraft painted in what must be one of the most flattering colour schemes seen on a DC-3. *AJB*

Right:
The C-47A N3239T flies with Valiant Air Command from Tico, close to Cape Canaveral in Florida, and was photographed during the annual VAC Air Show held in April of 1992. Acquired from the Danish Air Force as K-684, she previously flew with the Royal Norwegian Air Force and the USAAF, having been built at Long Beach, California in 1943. A steady camera platform, the guys of Valiant Air Command flew us on a number of very successful photographic sorties during which a wide variety of beautifully restored warbirds formated on us. *AJB*

One of the Monroe County Mosquito Control DC-3s, N231GB, stands with the rest of the fleet at Marathon in the Florida Keys awaiting the approaching spraying season. It is March 1988. *AJB*

This immaculately polished C-47 N10801 operated out of San Juan International for Air Cargo America in 1979, alongside the equally immaculate Caribou N544Y. It was previously with the Luftwaffe, as CA+014, for many years. *AJB*

Left:
Parked on the perimeter of Sarasota-Bradenton Airport, on the West Coast of Florida, this C-47 was looking rather the worse for wear amongst the flowers of a riverside garden. And Kilroy had been here too! *AJB*

Above:
It is March 1988. One of the Aero Virgin Islands DC-3s, recently acquired from Air BVI, climbs out of St Thomas whilst Four Star Aviation's engineers give their undivided attention to the port engine of their DC-3 N63701. *AJB*

Right:
Rival DC-3s eyeball each other on the ramp at Naples where they are undergoing maintenance in March 1988. The Eastern Express aircraft is having its starboard prop serviced, whilst N839M looks on.
AJB

RESS

Left:
Undercarriage legs creasing, N333EF gains altitude above St Thomas's runway as it climbs out for San Juan in the morning light. Four Star Air Cargo, who are based at St Thomas, fly this and four other DC-3s on freight charters throughout the Caribbean. *AJB*

Right:
Close-up photograph of the nose of N3240A reveals it to have been on the strength of No 721 Squadron of the Royal Danish Air Force, even though it is now operated by the Georgia Boys of Valiant Air Command out of Tico, Florida. *AJB*

Left:
More C-47s at Naples in March 1988. N840M on the left, has its engine cowls removed to reveal its Pratt & Whitney R1830s. The aircraft on the right is a mosquito sprayer. *AJB*

Above right:
On the visit in 1988, we found a pound full of retired aircraft at San Juan Isla Verde Airport, amongst them this Southern Flyer C-47 N45860. It was delivered to the USAAF on 27 May 1944 as a C-47C floatplane, the type being named 'Dumbo'. It was some 30kt slower than the conventional land-based model, and was even fitted with JATO bottles for Jet Assisted Take-Off to try to improve performance. It was modified back to a standard C 47A transport in 1944, and was based at Elmendorf AFB in Alaska before being civilianised. *AJB*

Right:
I found this C-47 N19906 stranded at Billings, Montana in June 1989 with magneto trouble whilst I was chasing fire-bombing A-26 Invaders. Belonging to Majestic Airlines, the aircraft had flown up from its base at Salt Lake City from where it ran a regular freight schedule. *AJB*

No, it's a joke really! This very smart C-47 was painted up to look the exact opposite for the film *Police Academy 5*. It was in the Hill Aircraft compound at Fort Lauderdale in March 1988, which, to my surprise, had disappeared without trace on my last visit in April 1992. The aircraft was registered in Santo Domingo as HI-445. *AJB*

Smart C-47 N2028 photographed on the Sekman Aviation apron at Miami in July 1980. We used to take our DC-3s up to Miami from the British Virgin Islands for wing pulls and major overhauls at Sekmans when I flew for Air BVI in the early 1980s, and there was always a kaleidoscope of propliners there to greet us on arrival. *AJB*

Working alongside five Short 330s, this DC-3-357 N29PR was flying with Air Puerto Rico out of San Juan in March 1988 when it was photographed in the cargo area. It is a Wright Cyclone powered aircraft, originally delivered to Delta Air Lines on the 23 December 1940. *AJB*

Photographed during the age of psychedelia at Opa Locka, Florida in 1977, this C-47 N9012 was operated by a travel club which specialised in tours to Mexico, hence the Quetzalcoatl down the sides of the fuselage of the aircraft. *AJB*

Left:
N8666 was operated by British Caribbean Airways out of Beef Island airport in the British Virgin Islands in 1982. The company was set up in association with British Caledonian Airways to fly their passengers down-island from San Juan. They also ran a Beech D18S for cargo flights. *AJB*

Above:
Back up in Belle Glade, in Central Florida on the shores of Lake Okeechobee, a fleet of DC-3s specialising in mosquito control and belonging to Environmental Aviation Services Inc, await the call. They may be able to quell the Mosquitoes, but the smell from the nearby sugar cane processing factory is another matter! Belle Glade is a 20/20 misnomer. *AJB*

Right:
Wearing the titling of Air South/Florida Airlines, N21768 lines up on Runway 27L at Miami International for a departure to Key West at the height of the season in February 1978. A right-hand passenger door version built for American Airlines in 1939, the aircraft latterly operated with Provincetown-Boston Airlines/Eastern Express as N40PB. *AJB*

air South
FLORIDA AIRLINES
N21768
H-16

Left:
Both of these DC-3s belonged to Carib Air Cargo and were based at San Juan International, where they were photographed in 1988. The farthest one, N87629, was the aircraft which ground-looped in St Vincent in 1985, was repaired, and flown home safely. *AJB*

Right:
Borinquen Air's DC-3, N18916, photographed at St Kitts (Golden Rock) in April 1985, not too far away from its home in San Juan. *AJB*

Borinquen Air

AIR
N2VM

Left:
Looking more like a victim of the breaker's yard than the result of a landing accident, N2VM of Air Pennsylvania leans in an inebriated stance on the field at St Thomas in the US Virgin Isles. The landing conditions at St Thomas are sometimes quite appalling,and this DC-3 could conceivably have been caught in a downdraught (note the flap position). March 1985. *AJB*

Above right:
N4577Z landing at St Thomas, against the backdrop of the mountain that is the cause of so much dangerous turbulence on the approach. N4577Z used to operate for Air BVI as VP-LVJ, until it was sold to Aero Virgin Islands. *AJB*

Right:
Another one of Four Star Air Cargo's DC-3s, N67PA, locked and chocked by the runway at St Thomas. *AJB*

Initially painted in the colours of Apple Air, with the registration EI-BSI, N3455 appeared at North Weald in the titling of Star Airways Inc, and was photographed there in September 1991. *AJB*

This DC-3-209B was delivered to Transcontinental & Western Air (the forerunner of Trans World Airlines) as NC14931 on 8 April 1939, and was photographed at Miami International flying for Proair as N14931 in March 1985. Its current status is unknown, as it was last known registered to the International Transfer Corporation of Seattle in 1986. *AJB*

AVI
N28346

Left:
N28346, a long standing member of the Aero Virgin Islands fleet, photographed on maintenance in its new colour scheme at San Juan in March 1988. A DC-3C, it was originally built as a C-49J. *AJB*

Right:
Undercarriage down, three greens, full flap, on finals for Runway 09L. N3XW is a C-47B owned by Air Miami Inc, photographed at Miami International in March 1988 slowing up the jets on the approach. *AJB*

Air Adventure

Left:
Air Adventures DC-3 N600JD parked at Fort Lauderdale in the spring of 1988 with N47CR in the background. Feeling adventurous? *AJB*

Right:
Literally hundreds of people were able to ride in Dakotas of all descriptions during the 50th anniversary celebrations of the DC-3 in 1985. In addition to the massive DC-3 festival in Canada, five of the breed met up in Europe at Eindhoven, in the Netherlands, in July of the same year, flying in from the UK, USA, Sweden and Ireland. They were hosted by the Dutch Dakota Association with their own immaculate DC-3 PH-DDA. Air Atlantique designed a fitting commemorative tail logo for the event, and flew us from Stansted to Eindhoven to join the crowd, with organisation courtesy of the Friends of the DC-3. *AJB*

783
Ready
4
Duty
DDA

Left:
R4D-6S 'Navy 50783' (N151ZE) of the Confederate Air Force was already there on our arrival, complete with Confederate flag and suggestive little nose artwork 'Ready 4 Duty'. *AJB*

Top:
The following day, we formed up a five ship squadron out of Eindhoven with PH-DDA as leader, and flew up to Schiphol. Here PH-DDA taxies out from the terminal to take up the lead position. *AJB*

Above:
N53ST was closest to us to starboard in the formation, and presented us with a target view *en route*. *AJB*

Left:
On our far right was the Irish, ex-Argentinian C-47, N4565L, photographed flying over the fields of Holland approaching Amsterdam from the south. It is such a shame that this aircraft is today lying at Ipswich in a derelict condition. So much hard work was put in by the guys in the Irish group. *AJB*

Left:
Fortunately, we were able to move around within the formation to photograph the other aircraft. Here is the Swedish group, the Flygande Veterane, with its DC-3 SE-CFP, which is now in full SAS colours. Photographed beyond SE-CFP is the R4D-6S, N151ZE. *AJB*

Left:
A shot through the windscreen of the Confederate R4D-6S and N53ST as we crossed the English Coast *en route* from Schiphol to Fairford. Our intention was to terminate the formation flight at the IAT meet at Fairford, with a flypast of the City of London on the descent. In the event, we flew the formation up the River Thames from Gravesend, over Tower Bridge, and then up the River to Kew and made a low approach and overshoot to Heathrow's runway 28R, peeling off right on a direct track to Fairford. We had lost the Swedish aircraft over the North Sea, as they could not afford to fly on to Fairford, but met up with the Aces High Dakota KG374 on the last leg of the journey to complete the five ship formation for our flypast at the destination. *AJB*

Retracting its gear in its unique asymmetric fashion, N80617 settles into the climb out of Beef Island in the British Virgin Isles, having delivered a cargo of fish. Belonging to St Maarten Traders, based in San Juan, this Dakota is equipped with oversize undercarriage doors which give it an extra few knots in the cruise. *AJB*

Devoid of its Air Puerto Rico titling, N29PR climbs out of St Thomas against the mountain that dominates the airport. The paved area seen just below the nose is a water catchment slope built to retain some of the small amount of rainwater that falls on this tropical island during the rainy season. *AJB*

Aero Virgin Islands operated this C-53 N331P for many years on its Caribbean inter-island services, eventually deciding to replace them with the Martin 4-0-4, but events quickly overtook them, and the airline slipped into receivership during the late 1980s. *AJB*

N38PB flares gracefully over the numbers at Miami International during March 1988 at the end of yet another flight down to Key West. *AJB*

EASTERN EXPRESS
N38PB
EASTERN EX
N35PB
EASTERN EXPRESS
N40P

Left:
A gaggle of Gooneys swirl on the Eastern Express apron at Miami International in March 1988, a year before their retirement and replacement with the Saab 340 and the Beech 1900. Unfortunately, even their careers were to come to an unpremeditated end with the demise of the whole Eastern empire at the end of the decade. *AJB*

Above right:
Sightless eyes gaze out at 180° over the airfield at Guadaloupe Pointe-a-Pitre in December 1982. These two ex-French Air Force C-47s lie derelict near the Air Guadaloupe hangar, having no doubt been a source of spares for their immaculate passenger DC-3s. *AJB*

Right:
The oldest aircraft by far in the static park at the Paris Salon in June 1991 was the beautifully polished DC-3 F-GDPP. This aircraft was one of the few remaining of the type on the French Register at this date. This is in contrast to an earlier period, when I began flying schedules there in 1968, when Le Bourget throbbed with the sound of their engines. It was one of the bases for the famous night mail service operated by Air France. *AJB*

Left:
The Soviet Union obtained a licence to manufacture the famous Douglas design, and built it as the Lisunov Li-2. Over 1,200 modifications to the original design were made, the most obvious being the Shevtsov nine-cylinder radials, here shrouded against the dust of Lanzhou on this Chinese example, taken in October 1986. *Mark R. Wagner*

Right:
South America stayed with piston engined airliners well into the jet era, and is home to the majority of the world's DC-3s. Here HK-140 of El Venado is on turnaround at Villavicencio in its native Columbia in February 1979.
C. J. Mak via Stephen Piercey

HK-140
El Venado Colombia

Transamazonica COLOMBIA
HK-1340
ARCA

Left:
Transamazonica are also based at Villavicencio operating three C-47s alongside an Islander and a Trislander. This one, HK-1340, was also photographed on the line on 15 November 1980.
C. J. Mak via Stephen Piercey

Above right:
The Columbian Air Force operates the airline SATENA, flying eight C-47s, two DC-4s and a pair of BAe 748s on an integrated national network based at the capital, Bogota. Here, the co-pilot drops the passenger steps as the skipper closes down the aircraft on arrival. Photographed in March 1975. *SP*

Right:
The Ecuadorian Air Force operated 10 C-47s when this picture was taken on 28 January 1977. They all carried dual military and civil identities, usually to help them with flight clearances when flying abroad. *Colin Ballantine via Stephen Piercey*

Based at Port Moresby in Papua New Guinea, Air Niugini operated a small fleet of DC-3s on aerial tours during the mid to late 1970s. Niugini is taken from the pidgin spelling of the country's name. *SP*

The neutrally orientated Finnish Air Force operated both C-47s and C-53s as transports, based in the south of the country. Here D-06 is was caught flying over home territory in August 1983.
J. Wegg via Stephen Piercey

This Royal Danish Air Force C-47 K-682 was a frequent visitor to Northolt, and was photographed there in May 1977, prior to being camouflaged. *Plane Fotos International via Stephen Piercey*

SE-BSM is a C-53, which began life with the USAAF, being transferred to the Royal Norwegian Air Force at the end of the War. It flew for SAS from 1948 to 1954 when it was sold to Sweden and operated with Linjeflyg and Transair Sweden before joining Swedair.
J. Wegg via Stephen Piercey

Preserved for posterity, the ex Swiss Air Lines DC-3 HB-IRN is mounted in the take-off attitude in a park near Kloten, Zurich.
H. U. Oehninger via Stephen Piercey

And still they go from strength to strength! Farnborough '92 saw these competing turbo-prop conversions facing each other in the static park, the South African contender facing Basler's much modified Turbo-67.
AJB

Right:
The ultimate advancement on the C-47 airframe was the much beefier Douglas C-117 with uprated Pratt & Whitney engines. One hundred examples were re-engineered by Douglas for the US Navy, and some found their way into civilian use upon their military retirement, this one flying out of Toronto for Millardair in September 1985. *G. Finch*

Below right:
And the tailpiece, could this be a wingletted DC-3? No, it's only a crease in the engineer's tour jacket! The 'Three' will be 60 years old in 1995, and that will be yet another excuse to kick the tyres, light the fires, and air some more airframes in the world's skies. *AJB*

TAILPIECE:

John and Maureen Woods of the Friends of the DC-3 are enlisting help in the organisation of the 1995 DC-3 anniversary celebrations. If you are interested, please contact them at 3 Dalcross, Crown Wood, Bracknell, Berks, RG12 3UJ. Telephone (0344) 56774. This could be your chance to get involved with the real thing!

Jess Ward